Starstruck!

Written by Quentin Flynn

Illustrated by Peter Townsend

Contents | Page

Starstruck!

With these characters ...

Cindy

Simon

Mean Bart Brannigan (Marcus)

Lone Star Lisa (Sheree)

"I am the real

Setting the scene ...

Cindy and Simon are making a video to enter in the video competition at school. Cindy is the director and Simon is the camera man.

Their two stars become starstruck. When they start behaving badly, Cindy and Simon need to do something — fast! The final video is a big hit — but it's not what their stars expected!

star of the video!"

Chapter 1.

Mean Bart Brannigan pulled his black cowboy hat down low. His black bandanna fluttered in the wind. His mean-looking eyes stared ahead. He chewed on a piece of straw.

Behind him, the people looked scared. Something bad was about to happen. *Real* bad.

“Cut!” yelled the director. Cindy stood up from her director’s chair. This was the first day of taping for the school video competition.

“Special effects! Hurry over to Bart. We need more dust!” she shouted. Two children rushed over to Bart. They waved large sheets of cardboard. Clouds of dust blew up.

“Action!” called out Cindy.

Simon pressed the green button on the video camera. Mean Bart Brannigan sputtered as clouds of dust blew up his nose.

"Stop!" he sputtered. "I can't breathe! And how will the audience see me in this cloud of dust? *I* am the star." He patted the dust off his shirt.

Sitting beside Cindy, Sheree made an angry-looking face. She was dressed up as a cowgirl with tall boots that were too long for her legs.

"Marcus is *not* the star," she said, tapping Cindy. "I am the one everyone wants to see in this video."

Cindy felt her head. She had a headache.

This time Marcus made an angry-looking face at Sheree. "That's not true," he replied. "And call me Mean Bart Brannigan while the camera is on!"

"Cut! Cut!" yelled Cindy. Simon pressed the red button to stop the video camera.

"Stop behaving badly or we'll never get this video finished!" said Cindy angrily.

Chapter 2.

Cindy told Marcus to swagger up the street away from Lone Star Lisa. Marcus walked up the street with his legs too wide apart.

"Now this is your scene, Sheree," called out Cindy. "You're Lone Star Lisa, and you're very angry with Mean Bart Brannigan. Action!"

The video camera began taping again. Lone Star Lisa stared angrily into the camera and wagged her finger.

"Mean Bart Brannigan! You are a mean man!" she growled. "Leave this town forever or I'll . . ." She stopped and shook her head.

"Stop! Bring the camera closer to my face," she said. "Everyone will want to see me up close. *I* am the real star of this video!"

Marcus grumbled. Cindy groaned. Simon just turned off the camera again. Making this video was becoming a nightmare. Everyone else couldn't believe how badly Sheree was behaving.

Lone Star Lisa said her lines once more. Her face filled the video screen.

Cindy looked at her watch. "OK, everyone. Today's taping is over. We'll meet here tomorrow afternoon at 3:30," she said.

The next day after school, the actors and the crew met once more. Simon put a new videotape in the camera and checked the lens and batteries.

"We're going to start with the fight scene," said Cindy to the group of "extras." "Mean Bart Brannigan and Lone Star Lisa are about to have a fight. I want all of you to look scared as you run for cover."

“Action,” called Cindy. The extras, acting as townspeople, looked at the camera with frightened faces. Suddenly, Lone Star Lisa ran in front of the extras, waving her arms.

“Stop! Wouldn’t it be better if I was in front of the extras?” she asked. “It’s a shame to start the fight scene without the star’s face up close.”

"CUT! Stop the fight scene!" yelled Cindy. This *was* a nightmare. She picked up a rope and handed it to Lone Star Lisa.

"You're going to lasso Mean Bart Brannigan," she said. "So let's do your lasso scene *now* and then you can go home."

"Good idea," whispered Marcus to himself.

Lone Star Lisa twirled the lasso and threw it. The lasso flew toward Simon.

Marcus ran in front of the camera with a mean smirk on his face.

"I think you should let me do this scene," he said. "*This* star knows how to throw a lasso!"

Sheree and Marcus glared at each other. The extras looked bored. Cindy slumped down on her chair. Another afternoon of taping wasted.

Chapter 3.

The next day at lunchtime Marcus walked over to Cindy and Sheree.

"I've got some bad news," he said. "I'm leaving. There can only be one star in the video and that should have been me."

"But you can't just leave after only two days. Please . . ." said Cindy.

"Sorry, but I won't stay," said Marcus. Just as Marcus was about to walk away, Sheree decided to tell them her news, too.

"I'm leaving, too. I've been asked to star in another video and I've said "yes". The kids in Room 3 know how to treat a star!"

Cindy was speechless. After only two days, her starstruck actors had ruined her video. She went to find Simon to tell him the problem.

"Don't worry. I've got a great idea," Simon said, smiling. "Follow me."

In the resource center, Simon walked toward the editing machine.

"What's that?" asked Cindy.

"This machine will help us edit our video," explained Simon. "We can also use it to take out the sound. And to add new sound."

For the first time, Cindy felt excited. They sat in front of the editing machine and went to work.

On the day of the video competition, the school auditorium was filled with students, families, and friends. Everyone was talking about who might win. The principal welcomed everyone and then introduced each video.

After each video, everyone clapped loudly. Simon and Cindy felt nervous as they waited for their video to be shown. Finally, the principal introduced their video.

When the video started, everyone was surprised. Lone Star Lisa was in the first scene wagging her finger. But it was not Sheree's angry voice on the video. The voice belonged to someone else!

Chapter 4

"Hey, you! Sourface Sam!" said the Lone Star Lisa voice. "You think you have the newest stiffest boots in the west. Well, you're wrong. I do!"

"But I'm supposed to be Mean Bart Brannigan," came a voice from the auditorium. Everyone giggled.

“Oh yeah, Whiny Wendy?” growled a voice that was not Marcus. “My boots are so stiff I have to walk like this.” Sourface Sam swaggered strangely down the street.

"That's hilarious!" laughed someone in the audience.

"Whiny Wendy? That's not hilarious!" squealed Sheree feeling quite upset.

The close-up of Whiny Wendy made the audience laugh again.

"I'm going to take your boots and break 'em in, Sourface Sam," she growled.

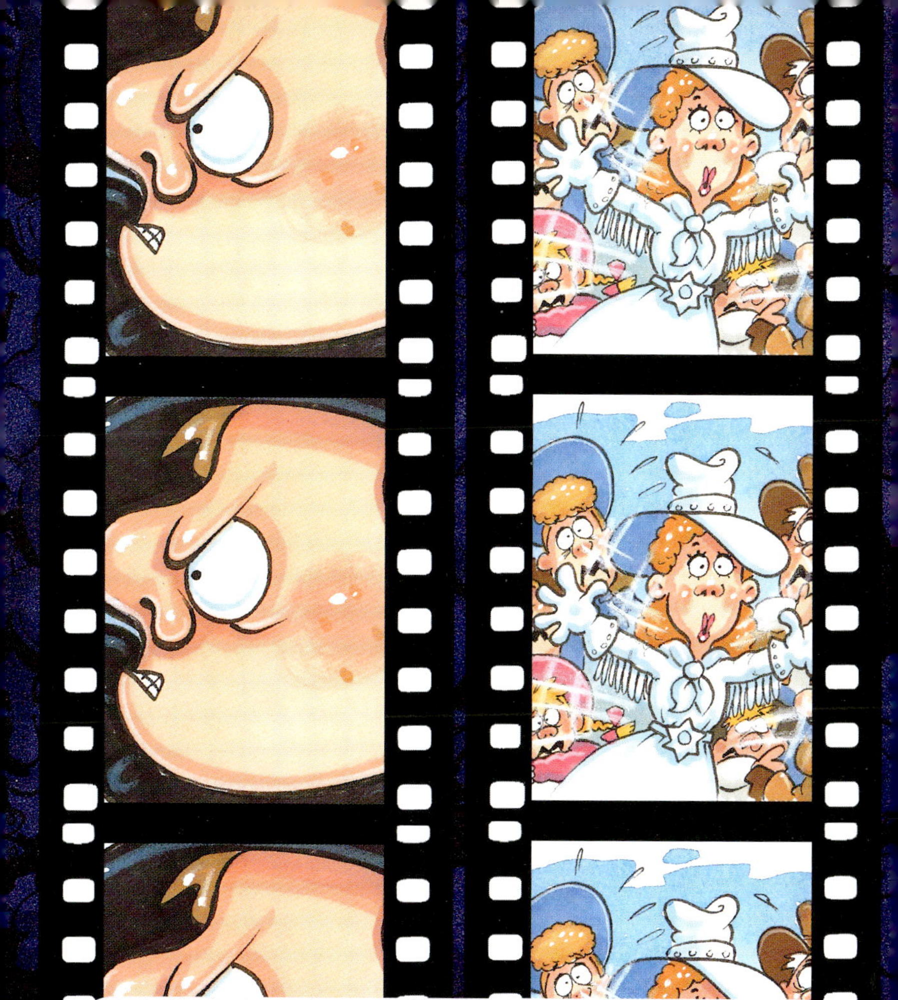

“I don’t want you breaking them in!” he said, making a face.

The extras ran away looking scared. Whiny Wendy waved her arms.

“Alright, Sam. Give me your boots!” she said. “Your boots look too new!”

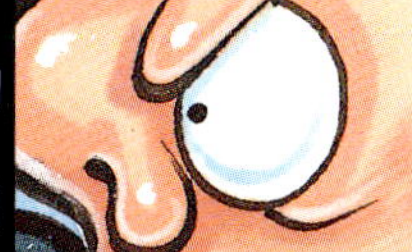

The audience couldn't stop laughing. This was the most hilarious video so far.

Clouds of dust blew over Sourface Sam. "I can't breathe!" he said.

Another close-up showed Whiny Wendy's face.

"Uh-oh," she cried. "His boots have started to leap off his feet!"

She twirled her lasso and threw it out of sight.

"Oh, no! Where are those boots?" she said.

Sourface Sam gave another mean smirk.

"So, Wendy. *You* have the newest, stiffest boots in the west now," he grinned. "But I've got something better."

“I have the dustiest shirt in the west!” he said patting his shirt.

The video ended, and everyone in the hall clapped loudly. Everyone except Marcus and Sheree. All they could do was squeal at each other.

“The winners are Cindy and Simon,” announced the principal.

Together they walked up on stage to collect their prize and make a speech.

"Thank you for the prize. Of course, we couldn't have done it without our stars!" Cindy said in her speech.

"Or without an editing machine!" whispered Simon.

"A Funny New Video"

While making a video,
Two stars do fight.
Both stars are wrong,
No one is right.

Then when both stars walk out,
It becomes very clear,
The cameraman and director
Need a clever idea.

With some smart thinking,
And some video tricks,
A funny new video
Now looked very slick.

On competition day,
To the two stars' surprise,
A video is shown
That they don't recognize.

They both look quite silly,
But it serves them both right!
When working together,
You must learn *not* to fight!